PICTURE A COUNTRY

Germany

Henry Pluckrose

W
FRANKLIN WATTS
A Division of Grolier Publishing
NEW YORK • LONDON • HONG KONG • SYDNEY
DANBURY, CONNECTICUT

7816978

This is the German flag.

First published by Franklin Watts 1998

First American edition 1998 by
Franklin Watts
A Division of Grolier Publishing
90 Sherman Turnpike
Danbury, CT 06816
Visit Franklin Watts on the Internet at:
http://publishing.grolier.com

Library of Congress Cataloging-in-Publication Data
Pluckrose, Henry Arthur.
 Germany / Henry Pluckrose.
  p. cm. -- (Picture a country)
 Includes index.
 ISBN 0-531-11504-6 (lib. bdg.)   0-531-15363-0 (pbk.)
 Summary: Text and illustrations provide an introduction to the
people of Germany and their lifestyles, as well as to the country's
geography, weather, and cities.
 1. Germany--Juvenile literature. [1. Germany.] I. Title.
II. Series: Pluckrose, Henry Arthur. Picture a country.
DD17.P6 1998   97-40861
942--dc21   CIP
                                         AC

Printed in Great Britain

Series editor: Rachel Cooke
Series designer: Kirstie Billingham
Picture research: Juliet Duff

Photographic acknowledgements:

Cover: Top SOA(All Over Bild Archiv/Wilfried Gohsens),
bottom left Getty Images (Robert Everts), bottom right
Getty Images (Bob Krist).

AKG, London pp.10, 14, 25 bottom;
Getty Images pp. 8 (Oldrich Karasek), 12 (Ed Pritchard),
13 (Hideo Kurihara), 15 (Marcus Brooke), 19 (John
Wyand), 28 (Bob Krist), 29 (Robert Everts);
Robert Harding Picture Library pp. 16, 17, 18, 24, 27;
The Image Bank p.25 top;
SOA pp 9 (All Over Bild Archiv/Erik Chmil), 20 and
21 (Gudrun Petersen/Joker), 22 (All Over Bild
Archiv/Wilfried Gohsens), 23 (All Over Bild Archiv/Udo
Kroner), 26 (All Over Bild Archiv/Josef Beck);
Travel Ink p.11 (Andrew Cowin).

All other photography by Steve Shott.
Map by Julian Baker.

Contents

NORTH SEA

BALTIC SEA

POLAND

Hamburg

River Elbe

Berlin

Brandenburg

NETHERLANDS

Weser River

Hameln

Rothenburg

Rhine River

GERMANY

Dresden

BELGIUM

Bonn

Mosel River

Kaub

Frankfurt

CZECH REPUBLIC

Trier

Stuttgart

Danube River

FRANCE

BADEN-WÜRTTEMBERG

BAVARIA

Munich

Bavarian Alps

Oberammergau

Zugspitze

AUSTRIA

SWITZERLAND

Where Is Germany?

This is a map of Germany.
Germany is a large country
in the middle of Europe.

Here are some German
stamps and money.

German money is counted
in deutsche marks.

This is a view of Zugspitze, Germany's highest mountain.
It is 9,721 feet (2,963 m.) high and is in the Bavarian Alps.

The German Landscape

Germany has many different types of landscape. In the center and the south, there are hills covered with forests and high mountains. In the north, the land is much flatter.

In winter, the weather is cold. Summers are usually dry and hot.

The German People

People have lived in Germany
for thousands of years. Today,
over 81 million people live in Germany.

In recent times, people from other
countries—for example, Turkey and Italy—
have moved to Germany to find work.

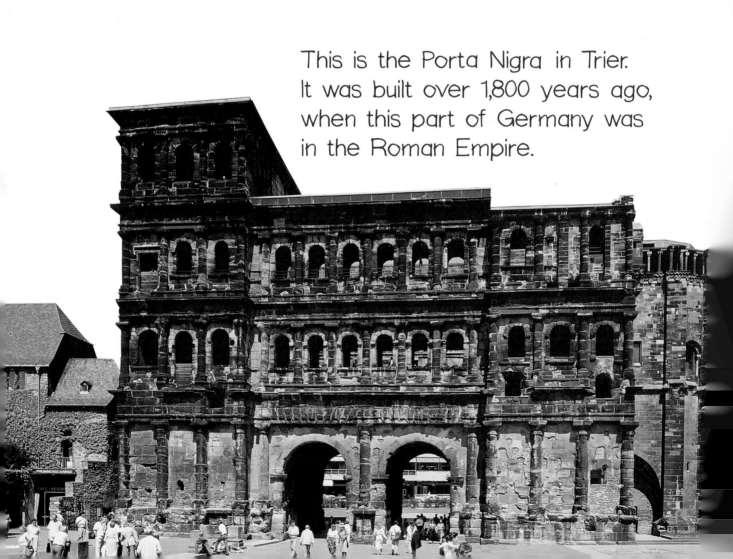

This is the Porta Nigra in Trier.
It was built over 1,800 years ago,
when this part of Germany was
in the Roman Empire.

This busy street is in Brandenburg in eastern Germany.

Where They Live

Most German people live in cities—Bonn, Dresden, Frankfurt, Hamburg, Munich, Stuttgart.

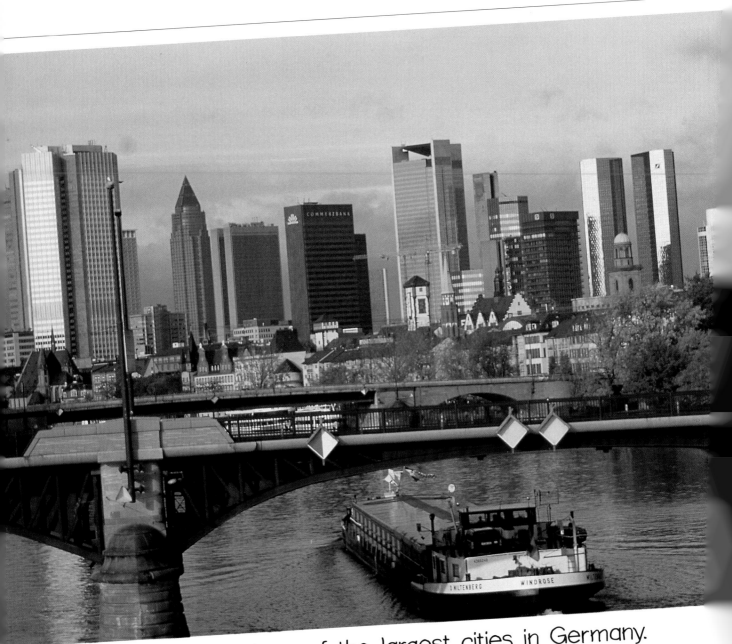

This is Frankfurt, one of the largest cities in Germany.

Tourists like to visit Rothenburg in eastern Germany to see its old houses.

Other Germans live in smaller towns and villages.

The Capital City

Berlin is the capital of Germany. Over 3 million people live there. Berlin is a city of wide roads, beautiful buildings, museums, and parks.

This is the Charlottenburg Palace in Berlin.

You can see Kaiser Wilhelm Church through this modern sculpture in the center of Berlin.

Goods to Sell

Germany makes and sells many of the things we use—from washing machines and cars to the lenses used in telescopes.

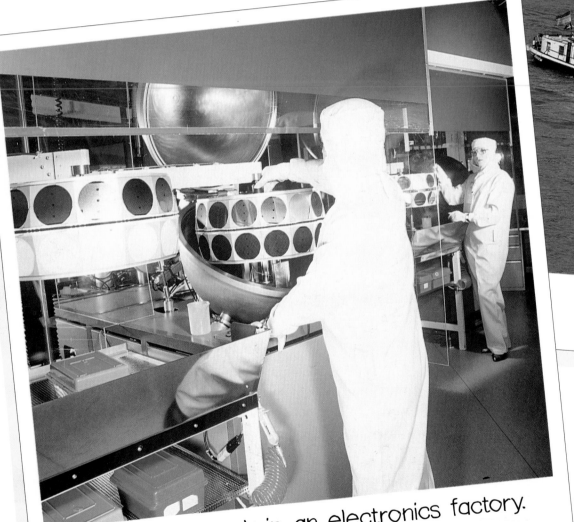

These people work in an electronics factory. They are wearing protective clothing.

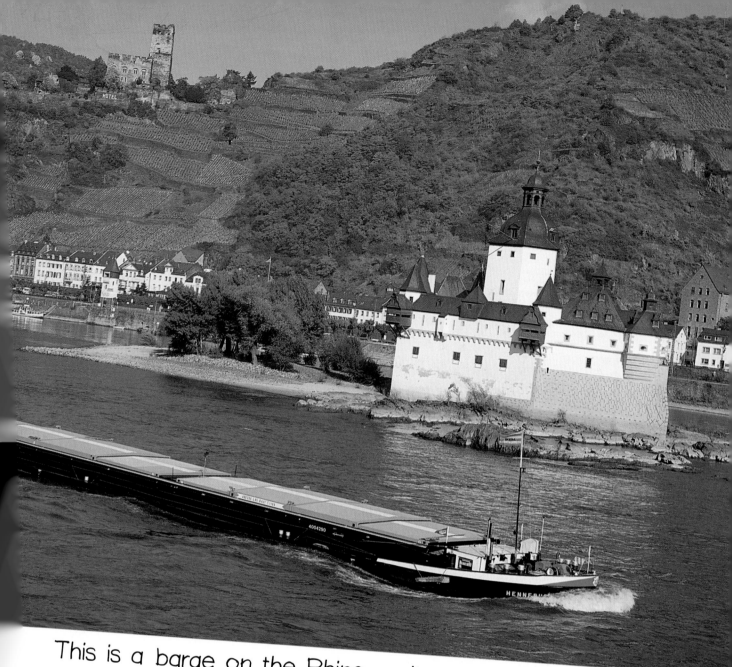

This is a barge on the Rhine as it passes through Kaub.

The Rhine River is the busiest waterway in Europe. The barges carry German goods to and from the huge port of Rotterdam in the Netherlands.

This modern German farm is in Bavaria.

Farming

German farmers grow many kinds of food—wheat for flour, hops for making beer, grapes for making wine.

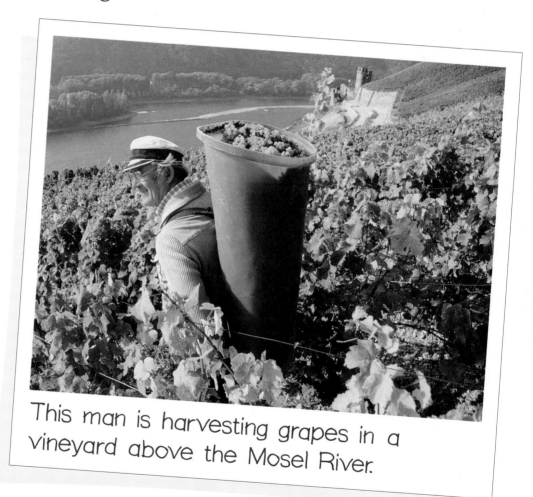

This man is harvesting grapes in a vineyard above the Mosel River.

In the south, they grow fresh fruit—apples, pears, and plums.

Family and Home

These two pictures show
a German family at home
and out shopping together.

German children spend their time very much as you do. They go to school, watch television, play games, and have vacations.

German Food

Germans enjoy all sorts of food. If you visit Germany, you might be offered hamburger rolled in cabbage, spiced sausages, bread dumplings, clear soup, salted herrings, and cakes made of chocolate, almonds, and cream.

Out and About

Germans play many sports. German teams have been world champions in soccer, tennis, and skating.

Water sports are popular in Germany.

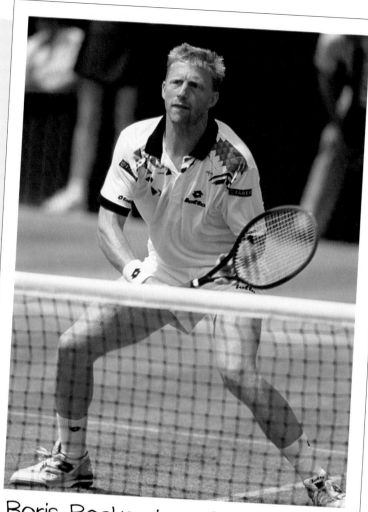

Boris Becker is a German
tennis champion.

Germans also enjoy music
and going to concerts.
This statue shows Beethoven,
a famous German composer.
A composer is someone who writes music.

German Festivals

There are many festivals held in German towns and villages, with dancing, music, and plays.

Every 10 years, the people of the town of Oberammergau act out the story of Jesus.

Every summer, crowds in Hameln watch a play about the Pied Piper of Hameln.

Visiting Germany

Many tourists visit Germany. They go to enjoy its beautiful countryside, its old towns, its music festivals, its museums, and its sports.

This is Sigmaringen Castle in Baden-Württemberg.

Index

About This Book

The last decade of the 20th century has been marked by an explosion in communications technology. The effect of this revolution upon the young child should not be underestimated. The television set brings a cascade of ever-changing images from around the world into the home, but the information presented is only on the screen for a few moments before the program moves on to consider some other issue.

Instant pictures, instant information do not easily satisfy young children's emotional and intellectual needs. Young children take time to assimilate knowledge, to relate what they already know to ideas and information which are new.

The books in this series seek to provide snapshots of everyday life in countries in different parts of the world. The images have been selected to encourage the young reader to look, to question, to talk. Unlike the TV picture, each page can be studied for as long as is necessary and subsequently returned to as a point of reference. For example, a German festival might be compared with the one in their own area; a discussion might develop about the ways in which food is prepared and eaten in a country whose culture and customs are different from their own.

The comparison of similarity and difference is the recurring theme in each of the titles in this series. People in different lands are superficially different. Where they live (the climate and terrain) obviously shapes the sort of houses that are built, but people across the world need shelter; coins may look different, but in each country people use money.

At a time when the world seems to be shrinking, it is important for children to be given the opportunity to focus upon those things that are common to all the peoples of the world. By exploring the themes touched upon in the book, children will begin to appreciate that there are strands in the everyday life of human beings that are universal.